CW01081845

Creating your own Web site

CASSELL&CO

First published in the United Kingdom in 2000 by Hachette UK

ISBN 1 84202 058 7

Designed by Chouka / Typeset in Sabon MT / Printed and bound in Germany

English translation by Prose Unlimited

Concept and editorial direction: Gheorghii Vladimirovitch Grigorieff

Additional editorial assistance: Simon Woolf, Derek Penfold, Jeremy Smith

A CIP catalogue for this book is available from the British Library.

Hachette UK

Cassell & Co

The Orion Publishing Group

Wellington House

125 Strand

London

WC2R 0BB

Table of Contents

Introduction

Introduction

The Web today is a world-wide phenomenon and is expanding by the minute. Back in the 1960s, this so-called 'Network of Networks' consisted of just a few slender threads linking military complexes, research centres and universities. The World Wide Web as we know it today surfaced only in 1993 when the Internet began to be opened up for everybody to use; not just official organisations, but also commercial companies and private individuals.

Today, the Web could just as well be compared to a beehive or an anthill, because rather than being the fruit of the efforts of a single spider spinning its threads in solitude, it is the result of the collective effort of the millions of people around the world who are online every day.

The Web is not only getting bigger, but it is also getting better every day, as software is refined, new technologies are developed and it seems as though the list of things you will be able to do on the Web will be limitless. The days when it could only be used to transfer dull old text items are rapidly becoming a distant memory. The Web is already a multimedia universe, teeming with colours and sounds, information technology has truly donned all its finery and is strutting its stuff in style. Art, fashion, design and music have invaded the Web to the delight of one and all.

Finally, because the Internet is by definition intended to be interactive, cosmopolitan and democratic, it has become accessible to all. The forbidding and elitist technological barrier that it once put up has been broken down and today the Web is a network that links a world-wide community in a universe of image and sound. We can all be a part of it if we wish. So if, after having cruised around the Web sites of the world, you feel its time to make your presence felt and grab your own little bit of cyberspace, why not create your own Web site? If that's what you'd like to do, then this little book will show you how.

Why a Web site...
and why FrontPage
Express?

Why a Web site ... and why FrontPage Express?

Who is this book for?

The answer is, for everyone interested in creating a Web site. The purpose of the book is not to provide an exhaustive treatise on the subject, but rather an introduction on how to create Web pages that is practical, free, and hands-on.

Practical

By reading this book you should be able to apply the knowledge that you gain directly, without requiring any exterior tuition. That is why although other Web editors are mentioned on pages 34-43, only one is dealt with in depth, namely Microsoft's FrontPage Express. The functions of this software application are explained step by step, illustrated by screen captures, so that you can proceed at your own pace. To make the experience as useful as possible, a real site will be created as you progress through the book.

Free

This book will enable you to create a Web site from design to publication without spending a penny.

FrontPage Express is included in Windows 98, and in the Appendix, you'll find the Internet addresses of access providers, host servers and others that include ancillary software that comes free of charge.

Hand-on

This book adopts a hands-on approach as knowledge derived from task-based learning can be applied directly. Best, and perhaps most surprising of all, you need no prior knowledge or experience to create Web sites.

The aim is to turn you into a 'budding Webmaster', not the finished article. You may find you may want to delve into the subject in greater depth, or simply update your skills at a later date, but you will have acquired a solid base upon which to build.

Why should you want to create a Web site?

Everybody has at least one good reason for wanting to create a personal Web page or site. You may have a particular cause to defend, a passion to share, some information to publish, or you may simply wish to get in touch with other people and show what you can do. Most people at least want to talk and exchange ideas and information with like-minded others. Creating a Web page means creating your own window on the world and your own fifteen minutes of fame.

If you have a magnificent collection of exotic butterflies, matchboxes or coins, you needn't let them collect dust on a shelf or idle in a drawer. If you are a photographer, musician or silkscreen artist, for example, you can show your work on the Web. If you have been through an incredible experience, a romantic love story, or if something comical has happened to you, why not share it with others?

The Web is a vast democracy, created by and for all, without any real supervisory body. To keep it that way, a number of rules have gradually come into force which form a code of conduct known as 'Netiquette'. These unwritten rules are essentially a matter of tolerance, patience and courtesy, so if you stick to these basic principles, you won't go far wrong.

ALI BABA
AND THE MILLION THIEVES

For surfers of the Web, the Net is a real Ali Baba s Cave, tee-ming with treasures. It has images by the million, pulsating music, thousands of amusing cartoons, animated logos and a host of small applications that enrich Web pages and make browsing such fun. Remember however, that not all are free. Unless explicitly specified to the contrary, you cannot just help yourself without asking. Both the real AND the virtual world are subject to copyright laws. Appearances can be misleading. The Internet is not a totally free market. You can draw inspiration from it, but shouldn t steal. On the other hand, if you really are tempted, you can always contact the author of the site that contains the particular item you covet and admire and ask him or her for permission to use it. However, many a bootleg site will offer you the opportunity to download music, games or other proprietary software which have fallen off the back of a virtual lorry. Beware! If you do, you will be breaking the law.

WORLD WIDE WEB
OR WORLD WIDE WASTE ?

Quality is the keyword here. No one wants to log on to a site that offers no information, aesthetic pleasure, or other reward. Similarly, one of the great features of the Web is that it is a constantly changing universe, so it s better not to leave pages containing outdated information on the Net, update them as often as you can. Also remember to check the spelling in your site. People who are familiar with computers and the Internet tend to scoff at those who aren t and call them computer illiterate . However, if the contents of some sites are anything to go by, it s a distinct case of the pot calling the kettle black. However much of a rush you may be in to get your page on the Internet, it is always worth spending an extra few minutes checking through what you are about to post before going ahead. First impressions count on the Web just as they do elsewhere, after all.

Other aspects of quality control are discussed later in the book, but many of these will appear self-evident as you gain experience surfing the Web.

Web site design software: the HTML editor

Though it may not look like it, when viewing an all singing all dancing version, the basis of a Web site is simply lines of programming code in HTML (HyperText Markup Language). Creating a document in any language requires software capable of managing it, i.e. software that 'speaks' that language. Software that 'speaks' HTML has existed since HTML was created in 1989, but it was not until the advent of the Web in 1993 and the Internet boom that it ushered in, that these HTML-fluent software applications began to proliferate and enter the public domain.

Software " in text mode "

These programmes are simple text editors, comparable to Windows Notepad. They have the disadvantage of being accessible only to 'specialists' for whom HTML holds no secrets and they don't show the result of the operations carried out directly on the screen.

On the other hand, they do have the advantage of total control of the code, thus avoiding unwanted surprises.

"Wysiwyg" software

FrontPage Express is a WYSIWYG (what you see is what you get) application. The underlying principle is to make it possible for you to create a document without going through the arduous task of learning an appropriate programming language first. WYSIWYG enables you to create Web pages, showing you the result you will obtain visually, without having to read through strings of elaborate text-based instructions. You can insert code by a series of very simple operations, mouse clicks, opening dropdown menus and so on.

 These editors can also be used to "retouch" the code manually, provided of course you are familiar with it.

Wysiwyg HTML page editors

There are many WYSIWYG HTML page editors on the market. These software programmes share a common goal, the relatively simple creation of Web pages, without having to tackle HTML, and the maximum compatibility and integration of these pages with the differing Web technologies.

As a rule, these editors enable you to carry out operations for which you would usually need to know the HTML tags, without having to enter a single line of code. The tags are entered invisibly by the WYSIWYG programme. Each action carried out on the screen corresponds to one or more HTML tags. So instead of typing out a line of code, you just need to enter the sentence and format it as you would do with a word processor, e.g. a font is selected from a dropdown menu, it is put in bold by clicking an icon on the toolbar, its colour is selected from a palette, and so on. More complex procedures such as creating tables are far less complicated with a WYSIWYG HTML editor than with a pure code editor.

FrontPage Express is the younger brother of Microsoft FrontPage, a software programme that has emerged as one of the most popular software applications for creating Web sites. It stands out among the myriad of software available on the market by being fast and simple to use. Unlike some of its rivals, it does not require specialised knowledge in graphics or animation. Those already familiar with Microsoft software will feel immediately at home with its interface and many different commands.

The other WYSIWYG editors

With the Internet boom and the general craze for creating Web pages (most Internet Service Providers offer 5MB of free Web space for this purpose), HTML (Hypertext Mark-up Language) editors are becoming more and more numerous, powerful and affordable. Among the vast array of software now available on the market some are gradually emerging as benchmarks in the industry. In truth, the choice of software for making Web pages is highly subjective and the best solution is to test the different tools yourself. Demo versions (which may only be used for a few weeks) can usually be downloaded from the respective sites of the various publishers.

Although FrontPage Express is a perfect starting point for those wishing to create a Web page, it is a relatively basic piece of software. As you learn, you will probably want to move on to more powerful applications. Some of the features that are not covered by FrontPage Express, but are highly useful to the new designer are covered below.

DHTML

DHTML, which stands for Dynamic HTML, combines two separate HTML technologies, cascading style sheets (CSS) and script languages (including JavaScript). DHTML makes it possible to insert dynamic elements into a Web page. These are listed below:

- Absolute positioning of objects on the page:

In software such as FrontPage Express, the different objects are arranged statically on the page and displayed by the browser in positions relative to each other according to the size of the window.

With DHTML integrated in some WYSIWYG editors, the different elements of a site (table, image, etc.) can be placed anywhere on the page, down to the nearest pixel (by displaying a magnetic 'grid' for example). Most of the time, overlays (GoLive, Dreamweaver, Namo Web Editor…) are used with this function.

These are floating layers that can be freely moved, duplicated, superimposed or saved as templates, etc.

Moving a picture in GoLive 4.

- Creating animated layers:

DHTML can be used to animate the elements of your site. In Namo WebEditor for example, the 'Chronology' window is used for this purpose. Dreamweaver has a nearly identical window called 'Scenario'.

Import an overlay from the editor in the 'Scenario' window by simply dragging and dropping it and assign to it to a movement on the 'Timeline' (linear movement, curve, etc.). The 'Behaviour' window provides a range of features that can be included in the animation (displaying a message on the screen, invoking JavaScript, loading an image, roll-over, etc.). It is possible to animate several layers simultaneously. The 'Preview in browser' command shows you how the results will look.

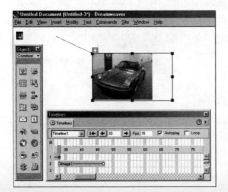

Timeline of
Dreamweaver.

- Creating Cascading Style Sheets (CSS):

Style sheets mean greater flexibility and speed in creating web sites. They separate the 'structure' (arrangement) of the different site components from their 'layout.' A style (font type, size, colour, bold, underline, etc.) is defined in advance in the editor through a specific menu. The style (or class) is saved under a desired name in '.css' (Cascading Style Sheets) format. From that point on, it can be applied to any portion of the text. Furthermore, the style can be edited and changed at will. However, remember that any changes you make will affect the entire text to which the style has been applied.

Stylesheet window in
FrontPage 2000.

Reactive images

Reactive images are used to define clickable zones within an image, i.e. areas with a link. Take the map of a country, for example. There you could click on the name of each town to access a description. If you were using a simple HTML editor in text mode, inserting such an image would be quite a complicated operation (you would have to create specific tags and define reactive zones by entering coordinates). In WYSIWYG software, however, this operation is carried out visually. In Dreamweaver for example, a clickable zone can be defined by drawing a circle, a rectangle or a polygon using the mouse and by establishing the link using a dialogue box provided for this purpose.

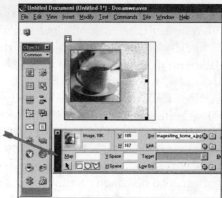

Toolbar for
the creation
of reactive images
in Dreamweaver.

Frames

Frames are used to divide a Web page into several separate windows. They are most commonly used to create a 'navigation bar', which, placed at the top (top bar) or the side of a page (sidebar), can be used to view the structure of a site immediately. This 'bar' is divided into different tabs, each of which leads to a specific page (by means of a link). The bar and the tabs remain in place irrespective of the page opened.

The Frames function is not available in FrontPage Express, although the software refers to it frequently (see the 'target frame' fields in link properties). All the editors described below can be used to insert frames in WYSIWYG mode. Some feature ready-to-use templates that can also be edited (Namo WebEditor, for example).

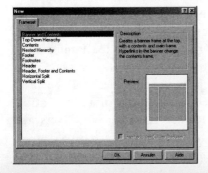

Namo WebEditor includes ten frame templates.

Site management:

Developing a site entails more than just creating it. You must also be able to check its code, make sure that the links work, update it, transfer it to a server, etc. Here is a brief survey of the features provided by many software programmes to help you carry out these tasks:

- Previewing in browsers:

This essential function saves considerable time. First, because you can switch back and forth from the editor to the browser with a simple click of the mouse and can thus see instantly what the pages created will look like. Secondly, because errors can be detected immediately. Finally, it allows you to detect instantly any compatibility problems. This is important, because the html tags used by some commands are not compatible between Microsoft Internet Explorer and Netscape Communicator. The attribute *blink*, which is recognised only by Netscape, deserves mention in particular. Sound files too are inserted into different browsers in very different ways (the tag created is *emded* for Communicator and *bgsound* for Explorer).

- Site map:

Thanks to a map or a plan of the site (Dreamweaver, GoLive), you can get a clear preview of the branching structure of your site, the internal and external links and all the files contained in the different pages (images, animation, sounds, etc). The Site Map also enables you to check and edit the links, and even to change their source. It allows you to edit the various files (pages, links, multimedia elements) with cut, copy and paste commands.

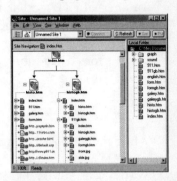

«Porsche» site map in Dreamweaver.

- Checking links

Even though the checking and editing of links is not carried out in a specific management window, these operations can entail a specific command (Claris HomePage). All the editors mentioned in this section can also clear the HTML code, thus deleting empty or redundant tags.

- FTP module: (See p.187)

An internal FTP module is important for publishing a site, but also for managing it. Updating can be done at any time by simply dragging and dropping in a window provided for that purpose (Namo WebEditor, Dreamweaver).

- Database management:

When the contents of a site need to be constantly updated (an agenda, directory, etc.), a database becomes indispensable. Editors like Claris HomePage provide help with connecting to a database. Using a database will save you a great deal of time, because when you can automatically make and edit changes using a form, you can avoid having to enter them manually.

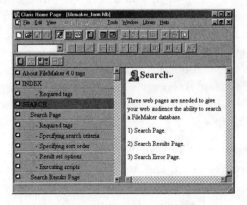

Forms creation assistant,
which includes FileMaker Pro databases.

Survey of WYSIWYG editors

```
1: FrontPage 2000 (Microsoft)
   http://www.microsoft.com
```

The new version of Microsoft's FrontPage, brought fully in line with the workings of Windows 2000, has corrected the weak points found in its predecessor. It has every right to be considered one of the most powerful and complete tools for making web sites. Intended for the mainstream, it is easy to get the hang of this piece of software which boasts a wealth of features and functions:

- FrontPage 2000 can be used to create as well as manage Internet and Intranet (local area network) sites. It features:

- Its own module for transferring pages to a dedicated server (FTP).

- A job sharing function.

- A structure display mode.

- Animation in DHTML through a wide range of effects.

- Cascading Style Sheets (CSS2) and overlays.

- 60 customisable subjects, including banners, buttons and wallpaper.

- Access database and form management.

- A Visual Basic script and Java Script editor.

- Furthermore, it is fully compatible with all Office 2000 applications.

Microsoft
Frontpage.

2: Dreamweaver 3.0 (Macromedia)
http://www.macromedia.com

Macromedia, the publisher of this software, has made a name for itself in the Web page creation world with a software suite, the ever so famous Flash (used for creating interactive animations), Fireworks (a vectorial image editor) and finally Dreamweaver, version 3 of which has just come out.

Although the latest version is quite expensive, the second version of this software can now be obtained free of charge when you purchase certain specialised magazines. Alongside FrontPage 2000, it is the most complete and most powerful piece of software on the market. Its complexity is such, however, that prospective users should already have some experience in creating Web pages, or else be willing to invest considerable time in learning how to use it.

Dreamweaver is the most innovative of all these editors. Every menu is accompanied by a specific floating tool palette for layers, animations, multimedia objects (including Flash animations), etc. A 'History' palette can be used to edit the various actions carried out (such as undo or save sequences of actions). Dreamweaver can be customised by every user to suit his or her needs. All the other functions mentioned previously are supported by this editor. In short, this tool is unbeatable when it comes to graphic design and it is therefore intended for professionals first and foremost.

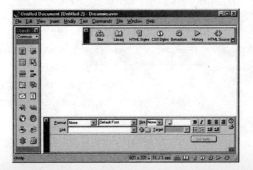

3: FileMaker HomePage 3.0 (Claris)
http://www.

The workings and functions of HomePage are reminiscent of FrontPage Express, but its additional features make it manifestly superior. These include an efficient page creation wizard, various site management tools, a built-in FTP module, style sheets, a rich library of customisable objects and, above all, the possibility of linking pages to FileMaker Pro databases. In spite of all this, some shortcomings, such as the lack of DHTML management, deprive this software of top ranking.

4: WebEditor 3.0 (Namo)
http://www.namo.com

Less well known than its competitors, this software is easy to master and has a clear, user-friendly look. It is an excellent compromise between an editor for beginners and a professional tool. All the functions a Webmaster needs (frames, style sheets, overlays, etc.) are built in. WebEditor has its own FTP module and comes with ancillary programmes such as a Gif Animator and image capture software. Finally, it features an array of more than fifty page templates that include animated buttons and banners.

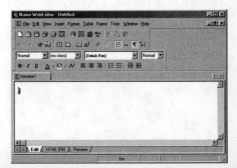

5: GoLive 4.0 (Adobe)
http://www.adobe.com

GoLive, recently taken over by Adobe, is gradually replacing PageMill, the Web page creation software from the publisher of Photoshop. This powerful, graphics-oriented software, contains a wide range of the most recent features (DHTML, style sheets, site map, etc.). It is not the easiest of programmes to get the hang of, however, and gives an overall image of being rigid. Having said that, GoLive is emerging as one of the most efficient WYSIWYG programmes on the market.

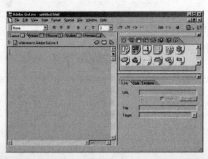

6: Netscape Composer vs. FrontPage Express

Just like its rival Microsoft, Netscape has included a WYSIWYG Web page editor (Netscape Composer) in its browser (Netscape Communicator). Available free of charge, this software has a look and feel similar to that of FrontPage Express, with a very similar interface and almost identical functions. You need to be aware, however, that there are no forms and no script editing features. On the other hand, Netscape includes its own FTP module, which is not available in FrontPage Express.

Hybrid editors :

To conclude this quick survey of WYSIWYG HTML editors, here are two text-mode editors that include some WYSIWYG elements, but do not have as visual an interface as the programmes mentioned above. They characteristically display simultaneously HTML tags and the various objects on the page, such as images. Often very efficient for editing code and scripts, they are intended for experienced users, who do not need the level of guidance provided by the other software applications mentioned above.

1: HomeSite 4.5 (Allaire) http://www.allaire.com

Although HomeSite is intended for seasoned designers, it has a WYSIWYG window, but you cannot do much with it. Its many options for site management and publishing facilities (in a wide variety of Web-oriented languages) make it an undisputed leader in its field.

2: HoTMetaL Pro 6.0 (SoftQuad Softwere) 152 Eur http://www.

This software combines display in source mode with automatic entry of HTML tags and a library that lets you quickly create dynamic buttons, style sheets, etc. A 'preview' mode lets you see the results of your work in WYSIWYG mode whenever you wish.

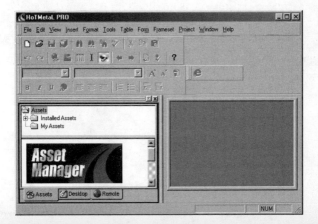

2

Creating your Web site with Frontpage Express

Creating your Web site with FrontPage Express :

Installing and starting up FrontPage Express

Installing FrontPage Express

Frontpage Express is available free of charge:

✍ as an add-on of Explorer 5;

✍ from the Microsoft Web site;

✍ by clicking **Start,** then *Windows Update* in *Windows 95/98.*

Needless to say, to download programs you must have access to the Internet.

To install FrontPage Express

1 Insert your Windows CD-ROM in the CD-ROM drive. You can choose to install all Internet Explorer or just Frontpage Express.

2 Explore the Explorer 5 folder and open the fpesetup.cab file.

3 Double-click on the fpe file and follow the installation instructions.

To startup FrontPage Express

To start up FrontPage Express, proceed as you would for any other software installed in your system :

Click *Startup*, then *Programs*, *Internet Explorer*, and finally *FrontPage Express*. The program window will open.

Note

Fpxpress

You can also create a shortcut on the Desktop, so that you don t have to go through dropdown menus every time you want to open the application. Go to My Computer, and follow the different steps that will lead you to the FrontPage Express file, which is symbolised by the icon shown above. Click this icon, keep the left-hand mouse button pressed, and drag it onto the Desktop.

Seems a little familiar?

Take a look at the screen on the next page. It gives you a summary of the different functions of FrontPage Express, which will be covered in greater detail later in the book.

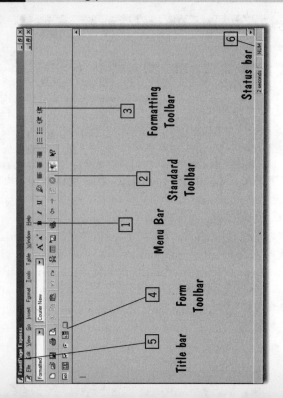

Title bar

Form
Toolbar

Menu Bar

Standard
Toolbar

Formatting
Toolbar

Status bar

1 The **Menu Bar** features ten dropdown menus:

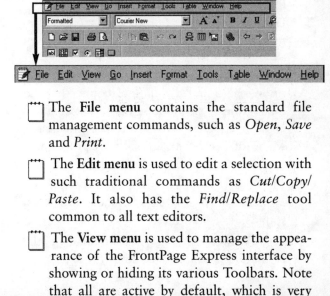

The **File menu** contains the standard file management commands, such as *Open*, *Save* and *Print*.

The **Edit menu** is used to edit a selection with such traditional commands as *Cut/Copy/ Paste*. It also has the *Find/Replace* tool common to all text editors.

The **View menu** is used to manage the appearance of the FrontPage Express interface by showing or hiding its various Toolbars. Note that all are active by default, which is very practical. This menu also features *Refresh* and *HTML* options, for updating the latest changes and for viewing the source code, respectively.

Go contains a series of direct links to the different pages opened in FrontPage Express as well as the different Microsoft Internet services - Outlook Express for sending and receiving e-mail and for connecting to Newsgroups; the Address Book that contains all your contacts on the Internet and finally, Microsoft NetMeeting, a software programme used mainly for videoconferencing.

The **Insert menu** is used to insert the main elements of your Web site, such as images, sounds, links and files.

The **Format menu** is used to manage the formatting and background of the text.

The **Tools** featured are: *Next* and *Back* to move through the different pages opened in FrontPage Express; *Follow the link*, which activates the selected link and finally *Font Options*, for choosing the default font for each type of character coding according to the different languages in which a Web site can be created.

The **Table menu** enables you to insert a Table and to edit its different items.

The **Window menu** features different ways to display windows opened in FrontPage Express.

The **Help menu** of FrontPage Express is very useful, but hopefully not necessary since you are using this book.

2 The **standard Toolbar** consists of a series of buttons, which are actually shortcuts to commands in the dropdown menus described above. Here, they are symbolised by icons. How these shortcuts are used will be described later in the book, when each of the relevant commands are dealt with in turn.

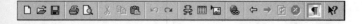

Once again, you will notice their similarity with other Microsoft software.

3 The **Formatting Toolbar** is used to format the text by means of buttons, without having to go through the dropdown menus. It is identical to the Format Toolbar used in Microsoft Word.

4   Finally, one last Toolbar deserves attention. This time, you will not be familiar with it, as it is specific to FrontPage Express. This is the **Form Toolbar**.

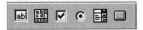

You have undoubtedly come across many forms on the Web, probably not least when subscribing to your Internet Service Provider and setting up an e-mail service. These forms are essentially questionnaires with various sections, or 'Fields', to be completed, checkboxes to tick, and so on. They are actually not that different from conventional administrative forms.

With this toolbar, FrontPage Express lets you insert all types of forms in your Web site by simply clicking. The different icons of this toolbar correspond to the different options of the *Form Field* in the *Insert* menu.

5   When you open the program, a new blank document is automatically created.

This document corresponds to the 'Normal Page' template that FrontPage Express uses by default when you create a new file. It is called 'Untitled Normal Page' – a name you can obviously change when you save the file. This information is displayed between brackets at the very top of the FrontPage Express window, in the **Title Bar**.

> **FrontPage Express - [Untitled]**

6   You may have noticed that the **time counter** at the bottom right hand corner of the FrontPage Express window has not yet been discussed.

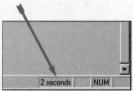

This function, very useful in theory but not very reliable in practice, is used when you create your site, and publish it on the Web, to gauge the time the visitors to your site will have to wait before the site is loaded in its entirety.

This information is crucial, as there is nothing more irritating than twiddling your thumbs while waiting for a slow page to be displayed. Web sites that are slow to download are often discouraging for surfers who are not convinced that the page in question is really worth a visit, so it is best to keep your site lean (in terms of Kb) and therefore easy to access, if you want to net a good crop of 'hits'. You can test the access speed to your site yourself, making sure you take due account of your connection settings, of course.

Most of the important elements in the FrontPage Express window have been covered so far, but if some explanations seem a little incomplete at this stage, don't worry. Their functions have just been outlined to date and will be explained further in due course.

You are now ready to transform yourself from a passive reader to an active Web page designer, so get ready to be creative.

3

Preparation

Preparation

Thanks to the WYSIWYG principle, creating a Web site is no longer the guarded privilege of experienced IT experts, or the infamous computer nerds. With FrontPage Express, creating a Web page is no more difficult than creating an elaborate document under Word.

 The degree of difficulty will obviously depend largely on the complexity of your site and the number and types of elements you want to introduce.

It is therefore prudent not to be too zealous at the outset. Be patient and proceed slowly step by step. If you don't understand what you are doing, you will not be able to understand your mistakes either, so it is wise to start by creating a simple site. You can always improve it once it is completed, as its first publication need not be final. The Web is a fluid and moving entity, not a fixed universe, and it is quite usual and even desirable, to update and improve your site on a regular basis, indeed some service providers will require you to do so.

Learning process

If you are an experienced Web surfer, you will have absorbed a great deal of information on your travels that will now come into its own. If you are new to the Internet, start by just surfing around some sites, browsing and generally getting to know this fantastic new world. Surfing the Web is often the best way to draw inspiration and give you ideas for your own site.

Bookmark or record in Favorites the sites you particularly like for future reference. There's no need to feel intimidated by the wealth of creativity that you'll find when surfing, or that total originality is the only recipe for success. All the great Web masters have followed the example of others at some time or other, so why not you. But don't forget the question of copyright (see page 16).

Getting down to the task

Before you begin, here are some tips worth bearing in mind:

Try and work out exactly what you want to put on your site in advance.

Have a clear idea of the look you want to give to your site, as this is as important as the content.

Go for consistency. Consistency between the different elements first, and then between the look and the content of your site. Aim to give your site a certain 'atmosphere', a bit of personality.

Finally, do not forego the use of paper altogether; a quick sketch can prove extremely useful at the planning stage. Write down the different elements of your page, sketch the layout and chart the areas that will contain an image, a logo, etc.

Put the different files you know want to use in your site (text, images, sound, etc.) in a single directory before you start. As you will see, you will have to send this entire directory to your host when you publish your site on the Internet (see Chapter 6).

A LITTLE FILING

The importance of creating a folder containing the various elements contained in your Web page cannot be stressed enough. It is useful to store the folder in the My Documents folder that is already present in the Desktop of all computers under Windows, as this is where documents that are imported into FrontPage Express will be saved by default.

Once this new document has been created, remember to file all the elements of your page in it as you go along. You can always subdivide this folder into subfolders when the different elements start mounting up, filing them according to function, such as graphics, sound, etc.

Avoid modifying or renaming folders, or moving files around unnecessarily. Each tag used to insert a file keeps the path that leads to that file in its memory. So if this path is no longer valid, it will be impossible to access files without providing FrontPage Express with an update on the new file structure.

I NAME THIS SITE...

The names of the different constituent files of a Web site are subject to numerous standardisation-related restrictions. These rules are the same as those that govern URLs (Uniform Resource Locators, the Internet address system).

So, don t include any spaces in your name. Use the underscore (_) if necessary to indicate a break between two words

(Page_2 , for example). The same applies to accented or uppercase characters. To avoid problems, you should stick to the 26 letters of the alphabet and the 10 Arabic numerals, and avoid special characters. Finally, rather obvious, but important, make sure you do not give the same name to two different files or confusion will certainly ensue.

Having taken all this on board, it is time to get down to the task.

To make the learning process more visual, and hopefully therefore more effective, you are now going to learn how to create a real site for the Web, taking as a theoretical example a Web devotee who is mad on cars and particularly in love with his Porsche 911, so much so that he wants to devote a site to it. Follow the steps on how to create such a site in this book and then visit the site on the Web at the following address :

http://www. multimania. com/thomisse/uk

Open FrontPage Express. A new blank document is created under the *Untitled Normal Page* template. The other templates available will be studied subsequently.

Save your page in the folder created for that purpose. It doesn't matter what name you give to it, so don't worry too much about this at the moment. This will be mentioned again later (see p. 186).

To save the file

Click the File menu, and then the Save As... command. Enter the name of the file in the 'Page Title:' field. You will have to change it subsequently, but again, don't worry about it for the moment. It will be dealt with later on. Similarly, don't worry about the 'Page Location :' field either at this stage.

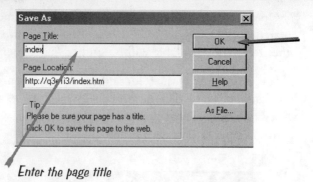

Enter the page title here

2 Now click the As File... button and then browse through your system until you reach the location of the directory of your site. Open it, then click Save.

4

The basic ingredients of a site

The constituent elements

1. Incorporating the text

The first step in creating the site is inputting the text. Generally speaking, the text will contain the core information you have decided to publish on the Net.

You may decide to use text that has already been written and saved in another word-processing programme such as Word or Wordpad. If this is the case it can, in theory, be imported into FrontPage Express, but it all depends on the format (the 'type of file' or 'extension') of your text file.

Explanations :

The only format for which FrontPage Express keeps both all the characters (with the exception of special characters such as accented characters, umlauts etc.) and the formatting, is '.txt', which is recognised by all word processors. Imported into FrontPage Express, files with the '.txt' extension can still be formatted with spaces and tabs (i.e. indents). Nevertheless, the styles (bold, font size, etc.) will have to be restored manually, you cannot use a style sheet created in the original programme.

With some of these programmes, (e.g. Microsoft Word) you can save text directly in HTML format. These files can be imported into FrontPage Express without changes, but you will no longer be able to change the formatting freely as the space and tab keys remain ineffective. Proceed with caution as you need to be sure that you will not want to change your text again.

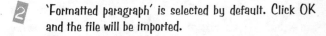

```
{\rtf1\ansi\ansicpg1252\uc1 \deff0\deflang1033\deflangfe1036 {\fonttbl{\f0\froman\fcharset0\fprq2{\*\panose
0202060305040502030304} Times New Roman;}{\f16\froman\fcharset238\fprq2 Times New Roman
CE;}{\f17\froman\fcharset204\fprq2 Times New Roman Cyr.;} {\f19\froman\fcharset161\fprq2 Times New Roman
Greek;}{\f20\froman\fcharset162\fprq2 Times New Roman Tur.;}{\f21\froman\fcharset186\fprq2 Times New Roman
Baltic;}}{\colortbl;\red0\green0\blue0;\red0\green0\blue255;\red0\green255\blue255;
\red0\green255\blue0;\red255\green0\blue255;\red255\green0\blue0;\red255\green255\blue0;\red255\green255\blue255;\red0
\red128\green128\blue128;\red192\green192\blue192;}{\stylesheet{\nowidctlpar\widctlpar\adjustright \fs20\lang2060\cgrid
\snext0 Normal;}{\*\cs10 \additive Default Paragraph Font;}}{\info}{\margl1417\margr1417\margt1417\margb1417
\deftab708\widowctrl\ftnbj\aenddoc\hyphhotz425\formshade\pgbrdrhead\pgbrdrfoot \fet0\sectd
\linex0\headery709\footery709\colsx709\endnhere\sectdefaultcl {\*\pnseclvl1\pnucrm\pnstart1\pnindent720\pnhang{\pntxta
.}}{\*\pnseclvl2\pnucltr\pnstart1\pnindent720\pnhang{\pntxta }}{\*\pnseclvl3\pndec\pnstart1\pnindent720\pnhang{\pntxta
.}}{\*\pnseclvl4\pnlcltr\pnstart1\pnindent720\pnhang{\pntxta )}}{\*\pnseclvl5\pndec\pnstart1\pnindent720\pnhang{\pntxb
```

This is what happens to a line of text
in Word when it is imported
in Frontpage Express.

Importing a file into FrontPage Express

1   Click Insert/File. Go to the directory where your text is located, select it and then click Open. If the file does not have an HTML extension, a window will list different conversion formats.

2   'Formatted paragraph' is selected by default. Click OK and the file will be imported.

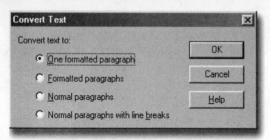

Note on Copy/Paste command

Unfortunately, this command is not very efficient if you are switching between FrontPage Express and another word-processing programme. Even if the selections are extracted from .txt documents, you may still get a nasty surprise. This command should therefore only be used to move text between files opened in FrontPage Express.

The other solution is to write the text directly in FrontPage Express. In general, personal Web pages don't contain a mountain of information, so the task should not be too tedious. Furthermore, with this method, you can avoid all the compatibility problems that arise when you are dealing with different text file formats.

Formatting under FrontPage Express

Characters

You can change the font, size, colour and attributes (italics and bold) of the characters of your text, and even give special styles to them.

 The 'Blink' style, which has the advantage of being rather eye-catching, but also the disadvantage of usually getting on the visitor' nerves eventually, does not function with Microsoft's Internet Explorer. It will only work if you are using the Netscape Navigator browser.

You can play around with these settings in several ways:

Before you type your text, open the *Format/Font* menu. In the window displayed, you can change the characteristics of the text you will write afterwards. You can see the result in the *Preview* area before you enable your choices.

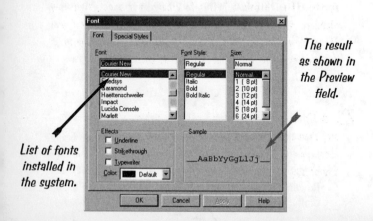

The result as shown in the Preview field.

List of fonts installed in the system.

The fonts

With FrontPage Express you choose a font from those installed on your system. However, if this font is not present on the machine of the person visiting the site, it will be replaced either by a similar font, or by a standard font of the operating system. It is therefore better to create your page using only standard Windows fonts, such as Arial, Courier, New and Times New Roman. On the Macintosh, Times New Roman is replaced by Times and Arial is replaced by Helvetica.

⚠ A title can also be created with a graphics editing programme, then saved as an image in a format recognised on the Web (see page 100) and imported onto your page using FrontPage Express.

The same operations can be carried out directly from the **Formatting Toolbar** by clicking on the corresponding icons.

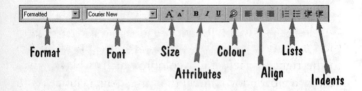

To edit text you first of all need to select it. Right-click on the selection (highlighted) to open a shortcut menu. Click the *Font Properties* option to open the formatting window described previously.

The same applies if you use the *Edit* menu or the icons of the *Formatting Toolbar*.

The choices for formatting characters, or letters, do not require further explanation, except regarding the choice of colour. Conventional colours can be used to define the structure of a piece of text and make the text itself easier to read at the same time, e.g. black for the main text with red titles. However, it is very likely that sooner or later you will want to deviate from the usual colour combinations and become a little more adventurous. You can choose the colour of a character string in the *Effects* field under the *Format/Font* menu. A button to the right of the default colour, which is black, gives access to a dropdown menu that gives you a choice of 16 pre-set colours, or the option to create your own customised colour.

To create your own custom colour

Click 'Custom', at the bottom of the colour menu. The colour window which appears comprises several fields: basic colours, custom colours (the palette here is composed of 16 blank boxes), a colour finder, a small preview field and the RGB (Red Green Blue) and HSB (Hue Saturation Brightness) of the active colour.

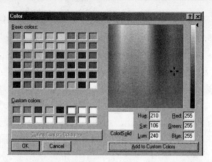

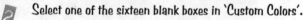

2   Select one of the sixteen blank boxes in 'Custom Colors'.

3   In the colour finder, click on the colour you want and adjust the brightness (with the vertical level on the right of the colour finder) and the other components using the keyboard (each setting can extend to 256 levels, i.e. select a value from 0 to 255).

4   Once you have selected the colour, click the 'Add to Custom Colors' button. Click OK. A new colour is created, and will henceforth be accessible in the list of custom colours, so you can use it again.

You can also select a new colour directly without adding it to the custom colours. The colour will change, but as it will not have been saved, you will have to enter the value of its different components manually if you want to use it subsequently.

You can style the text on your page in almost any way that you want. You can determine the appearance of titles, captions, the main body of the text and so on. The formatting options chosen for the text on a Web site are fairly important as they determine to a large degree its potential visual appeal.

Paragraphs

You can also edit an entire paragraph, either by attributing a pre-set paragraph format (or template) in FrontPage Express, or by choosing a type of alignment. These settings can be adjusted with the *Format/Paragraph* command or by right-clicking on the selected paragraph, or the corresponding icons in the *Formatting Toolbar*.

Example of templates in Frontpage Express.

How to select a paragraph

Place the mouse cursor outside the paragraph so that the insertion point turns into a white arrow. Single click to select a line; double click to select the entire paragraph. The selection is indicated in negative.

A horizontal line between two paragraphs or groups of paragraphs improves the spacing of the layout and makes breaks easier to see. In FrontPage Express you can access this function with the *Horizontal Line* command from the *Insert* menu.

The different settings of the inserted line can be adjusted by double-clicking on that line. In the *Horizontal Line Properties* box which then appears, you can change the width (as a percentage of the window or in pixels), the height, the alignment and the colour of the line. Finally, you can choose whether to retain the solid line effect (no shading).

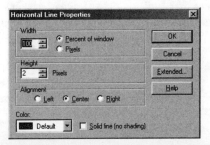

A horizontal line is deleted in the same way as any other piece of data.

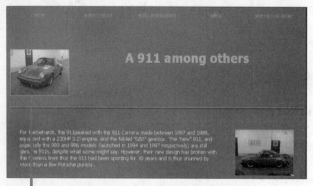

Every page title in the 911 site is separated from the rest of the page by a horizontal line.

Indents and indentation

You cannot use keyboard tabs in HTML language. In FrontPage Express, this command is attributed to two different icons in the Formatting Toolbar.

These icons are the same as those used for indenting in Microsoft Word.

Line break and new paragraph

The Enter key automatically defines a new paragraph. The line spacing between two paragraphs is greater than that between two lines. For a single line space, press Shift and Enter simultaneously, or use the Break/Normal Line Break command in the Insert menu.

The page

The properties of the current page can be accessed in *File/Page Properties*, or by right clicking anywhere in that page. The Page Properties window has four tabs.

Only the *Margins* tab is dealt with here here; the others will be discussed later if they lie within the scope of this book.

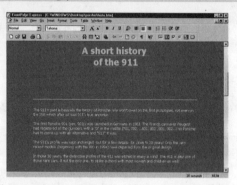

In this page, the inner and outer margins are fixed at 80 pixels.

The default margins created in FrontPage Express are 12 pixels for the left margin and 16 for the top margin, but you are free to change them.

Bullets and numbers

Bullets and numbers are used to break up text and give it a clearer structure. If your text is to be presented as a list, you can precede each paragraph or several pre-selected paragraphs with bullets or numbers. Bullets are tiny solid circles that indicate a new 'point' in your text. There are several different types of bullets in FrontPage Express. Numbered lists can use Arabic numerals, Roman numerals or letters. Other styles of lists are also available.

To put your text in list form

Select the different paragraphs you want to list, then open Format/Bullets and Numbering. Three tabs are available - Bulleted, Numbered and Other style. Choose the style you want and press OK.

Remove formatting

In the *Format* dialogue box, you can also remove formatting. If this is what you want to do, select all or part of the text and click *OK* to confirm.

TEST YOUR PAGE

The best way to make sure that you have carried out the operations properly when creating a Web site is to test the page as often as possible.

Save your page in the appropriate directory and then open your browser (you do not have to exit FrontPage Express) and the file you have saved. If you do not know how to do this, look in your browser s Help menu for assistance with opening a local file. Look carefully at the way your Web page looks on the screen, as you may find it s not quite what you had in mind. Try to understand what you did wrong, and go back and make the necessary corrections. Save the new changes and return to your browser. You do not have to open your page again. By clicking the Refresh command on your browser s toolbar, you will redisplay the page taking the latest changes into account.

2. Organise your page with tables

The *table* menu in FrontPage Express may prove useful if you want to:

Put your text in a box, so as to make it stand out in your page.

Create a table in order to structure the information you place on the Web in rows and columns.

Use tables because they divide a page into many independent elements which, when used ingeniously, will often make up for the shortcomings of FrontPage Express and even enhance its possibilities. We will return to this aspect presently.

Go to the *Table* menu and select *Insert table*. You can also do this by clicking on the icon shown here.

The *Insert Table* window has three different fields.

In the first field, *Size*, enter the number of rows and columns for your table. To create a simple box for the text, compose a table consisting of a single row and a single column.

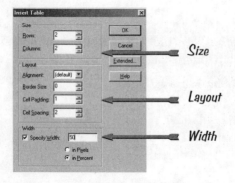

In the second, *Layout*, you can align the table on the page, set the border size (in pixels), the cell padding (or internal margins of each cell) and the cell spacing (the margins that separate the different cells).

In the third and last field, *Width*, you can specify the width of the cells (in pixels or as a percentage of the width of your page). If this field is not completed, the cells enlarge to fit as you enter text. The same applies to the height, as every new line will stretch the cell vertically.

Top speed	153 mph/245 kph
Power	170 kW/231 bhp @ 5900 rpm
Acceleration	0-60 mph in 6.0 sec
Torque	284 Nm @ 4800 rpm
Weight	1188 kg
Size	429 x 165 x 132 cm
Engine	3.2 litre 6 cylinder boxer
Tires	225/60 VR 15"

When you have entered your choices, click *OK*. The table will be inserted in your page and you can then complete the cells. Child's play!

To format the text of your cells, proceed in the same way as for any character string.

You can also create a table by using the corresponding line in the Toolbar.

Click this icon, keep the left mouse button pressed and drag the cursor to select the number of rows and columns you want for your table. Release the button when you have finished.

The greyed cells are selected.

To change the table layout

The *Table* menu features many options you can apply once your table has been created. These are quite clear and so don't require any further comment. Nevertheless, the last two need to be mentioned: *Cell Properties* and *Table properties*.

These two menus can be used to change the alignment, colour, size and other such settings, but also to customise and to liven up tables.

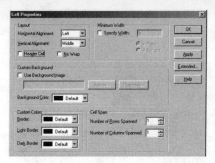

You can format either the entire table (through *Table Properties*), or a given cell (*Cell Properties*).

To select a cell, place the cursor in it. To select a range of cells, place the cursor at the edge of the table. It will then turn into a black arrow. Click, keep the button pressed and drag the mouse to select the number of cell rows you want to customise.

In *Custom colors* you can define the border of your table, which is set by default to the background colour.

Changing the colour of the border can give your table
the relief effect that is characteristic of Windows screens.

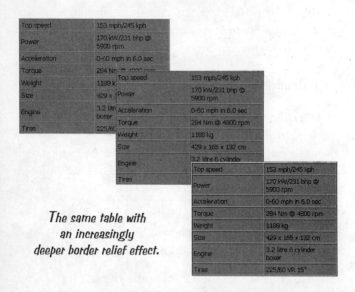

*The same table with
an increasingly
deeper border relief effect.*

Top speed	153 mph/245 kph
Power	170 kW/231 bhp @ 5900 rpm
Acceleration	0-60 mph in 6.0 sec
Torque	284 Nm @ 4800 rpm
Weight	1188 kg
Size	429 x 165 x 132 cm
Engine	3.2 litre 6 cylinder boxer
Tires	225/60 VR 15"

To delete a cell, a range of cells or the entire table

Select the different items you want to delete (as just described). Then press the *Delete* key or use the *Clear* command in the *Edit* menu.

3. Decorating your Web page

Inserting images in a site to customise the background, to illustrate the site, or to create a gallery is a good way of attracting the attention of visitors. It will liven up your site and make it more original. Unlike text, which has to be read, an image can be taken in at a single glance, thereby instantly drawing the eye of the surfer.

However, having said that, images in Web sites should really be used sparingly and with caution due to the time they take to download. A slow download may send a potential visitor to your site off to pastures new if he or she gets bored with waiting.

Apart from the speed of your Internet connection, the decisive element for transmission rate (the length of time pages take to download) is the size in megabytes of the image. This size depends on the resolution of the image, the number of colours (which depends on the type of coding) and the format of the image file.

Resolution

The resolution, or the quality and sharpness, of an image is determined by the number of pixels (small units of image) displayed on the screen. The unit of measure is not the total number of pixels, but the number of pixels displayed vertically and horizontally on the screen (e.g. 640 x 480, 800 x 600, 1024 x 768, etc). These values depend on the graphic performance of the computers, so they vary from one case to another.

Three aspects must be taken into account when creating Web sites:

The size of the image varies depending on the resolution of the screen.

An image with a dimension of 160 x 120 pixels will take up one sixteenth of the surface of a screen with a resolution of 800 x 600, but one fortieth of a screen with a resolution of 1024 x 768. Conversely, an image that occupies one sixteenth of the surface of this screen will cover one sixth of a 640 x 480 pixel screen.

Dimensions corresponding to the 'average' monitor resolution must therefore be used. This is subject to change, as the average level of equipment used by Net surfers gets ever more sophisticated. Nowadays, 800 x 600 can be considered a standard screen resolution.

The size of an image depends on its dimensions.

Each pixel forming part of an image contains a certain quantity of information that has to be stored. As the dimensions increase, so do the number of pixels. As an image increases in size, it will take longer to download. Keeping the dimensions of an image down therefore is crucial, as it reduces the amount of time it takes to access a site.

Resolution and quality

The quality of an image depends on the resolution of the computer screen. A low resolution displays a 'dotted', grainy image with jagged lines and a loss of detail. A resolution of 640 x 480 will allow you to display images of sufficient quality.

Colour coding

Each pixel can have a number of bits (binary units) associated with it. For a single bit (zero or one), there is a palette of two colours (black and white). This palette can be extended to 256 colours by using 8 bits for each pixel, and to 16.8 million colours by using 24-bit coding.

This last type of coding is known as true colour.

The size in kilobytes (KB) of the image therefore also depends on the number of bits on which the colours are coded.

Therefore, for an image with a resolution of 160x120 pixels, the size file will be:

160x120x1 = 19,200 bits, i.e. 2,4 KB in black and white

160x120x8 = 153,600 bits, i.e. 19.2 KB in 256 colours

160x120x24 = 460.800 bits, i.e.57.6 KB in true colour

The size of an image should not exceed 30 to 50 KB when composing Web pages. It is therefore better to make do with a palette of 256 colours.

The file format

An image can grow very rapidly in size, which is why graphic files used on the Internet are compressed. Compressing an image results in a loss of quality, but this loss will be not be too noticeable when viewing an image displayed on the Internet.

There are two standards that are used universally on the Web for compression: GIF and JPEG formats.

Compuserve's GIF (Graphic Interchange Format) compresses images on 8 bits maximum (256 colours), which is fine for compressing logos, window backgrounds and all images comprising wide large plain areas.

JPEG format (Joint Photographic Experts Group) can attain a compression rate of 1 per 200 KB and is coded on 24 bits (true colour).

Take as an example a photograph of 160 x 120 pixels, in 256 colours, saved in TIFF (Tagged Image File Format, i.e. non-compressed format). This photograph will use up 2.5 KB of memory, which can be reduced to 18 KB when the image is compressed in GIF or as little as 7 KB using the maximum compression rate in JPEG.

The **PNG** (Portable Network Graphic) format should also be mentioned. A recent arrival in the public domain and touted as the graphic format of the future for the Internet, it is still used sparingly. Similar to GIF, this format features a superior compression rate and can manage transparencies and 24-bit files. It is integrated into the most recent browsers and graphic data processing software. This format has been developed because the compression formula used in GIF is not in the public domain.

How to import an image into your Web page

If you have followed the instructions given above, you will now be ready to integrate an image into your site.

Save your image file in GIF or JPEG format in the your Web site's folder.

In FrontPage Express, move the cursor of your mouse to the place where you want your image to appear. Open the *Insert* menu and click *Image*. Click the *Browse* button next to the *From File* area. Go to the folder containing the files for the composition of your site, select your image and press *OK*. The image is now inserted. An icon in the *Toolbar* will spare you the effort of using dropdown menus.

You can get the same result using the *Copy* and *Paste* commands.

How to edit an image

When you have selected an image, sizing handles appear on the corners and the sides, and the image will be displayed in reverse video. You can access several formatting options via the *Image Properties* window. This can be selected through the *Edit* menu or by right clicking once.

The 'Appearance' tab has two areas:

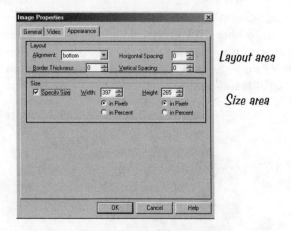

In the first, *Layout*, you can change the alignment of the image and frame it with a black border.

The alignment can be edited directly from the corresponding icons in the *Formatting* toolbar.

Notes

You can also create a far more elaborate frame by inserting the image in a table. Create a table with a single cell and then just insert an image to give it a border with a relief effect. The size of the cell will adjust automatically to that of the image. Now set the cell padding to zero, and the frame will adjust to fit.

You can customise the borders in the Table properties menu.

Dressing an image

The dressing of an image creates an invisible frame, a blank area around it that sets off text or other juxtaposed graphics so that the image can breathe on the page. An imported page is always dressed by default so that the text is not superposed on it.

In the lower area, *Size*, you can change the size of the image either in *Pixels* or in *Percent*. Note that the image is not re-sampled, so reducing the actual size of the image will affect the display on the screen, but not the size of the file in KB. To reduce the size in KB, use a graphics editing package or Windows Paint, if you have it.

If you wish to change the size of an image, you can proceed manually, using the resizing handles mentioned previously.

Alternative representations of an image

The *General* tab of the *Image Properties* window contains an area of particular interest. It is called *Alternative representations* and comprises two fields: *Low-Res(olution)* and *Text*.

To accommodate impatient visitors to your site, most HTML editors will suggest that you substitute a simplified or 'light' version of the image while it is being loaded and a brief caption of the image in question. Veteran Web surfers will already know about this 'alternative' (the usual name given to this function).

FrontPage Express makes this task very easy

 Create and save a light version of your image and use the 'Browse' button next to the 'Low-res' field to retrieve it. This light version, which should not exceed 2 or 3 KB, will be the first to appear on your site. It will be automatically replaced by the original version once the necessary loading time has elapsed.

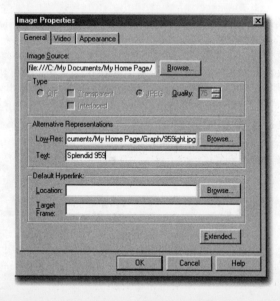

2   In the 'Text' field enter an explanatory comment on
your light version, which visitors can subsequently
access by placing the cursor on the original version of the
image (once downloaded).

*Alternative
text.*

*The same image
in a light version.*

Note

You can edit the quality of a JPEG image in FrontPage Express by adjusting the JPEG compression rate in the General tab under Image Properties. When you exit this window, you will be asked to confirm the changes made to the image.

Transparent and interlaced options

These two options in the *General* tab in the *Image Properties* dialogue box are available when dealing with the GIF format.

You can use the first to import a GIF file with a transparent background.

This feature helps to vary and enliven the appearance of your site by getting rid of the rectangular frames of pages. If you want to import a logo, a silhouette or any graphic cropped against a solid background, save them in GIF format, in order to attribute a transparent colour to the image. If this option is not available, you can use Microsoft Paint. The *Image/Attributes* menu has a field entitled 'Transparency' where you can choose a relevant background colour.

The interlacing or non-interlacing of a GIF file affects the way it is displayed on the Web. An image appears gradually if it is interlaced or 'in blocks' if it is not. The 'interlaced' option is selected when you save a file in GIF format.

The page background :

The default colour of every page created in FrontPage Express is white, but as in the case of characters and table borders, you can change this colour. You can even replace a solid background colour with an image, but you must take care that your background does not impair the legibility of your text, which is of prime

importance. Surfers who will take the trouble to deci-
pher muddled Web pages are very rare indeed.

Changing the background colour

You can change the background colour in five different ways:

Open the *File/Page properties* menu, select the
Background tab and attribute a colour (default
or customised) in the 'Background' field.

Right-click on your page to access its properties
through a shortcut menu.

Open the *Format/Background* menu.

You may also want to customise the colour of the
background. This colour is a salient feature of the look
you give to your site, so adapt the colour according to
your tastes, but remember to make sure however that the
text is still clearly legible.

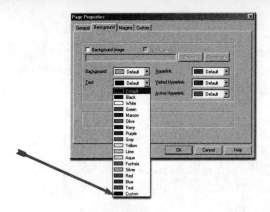

Access the background configuration menu and open the dropdown menu to the right of the *Background* field. The last colour on the list is called *Custom*. The way to create a custom colour has already been explained. (see page 79).

Insert a background image

The background can also be customised by inserting an image. To do this, tick the *Background Image* checkbox in the *Page Properties* windows.

A few points are worth mentioning:

It is preferable to keep the background fairly low key in order not to interfere with the text or the other images on the page.

Remember that your image must not exceed 600 x 800 pixels if you want it to be viewed in its entirety by the majority of surfers, i.e. without the need to use scroll bars.

When you opt to insert a background image, use the *Browse* button to access the contents of your hard disk. Go to the folder (directory) of your Web site, click on the image you want to insert and press *OK*. The path of the file will be entered.

Click *OK* again, and the operation is complete.

You have probably noticed that when your image does not take up the entire screen, it is automatically repeated until it fills all the visible space. This technique, which is used in Windows wallpapers, is known as 'tiling'.

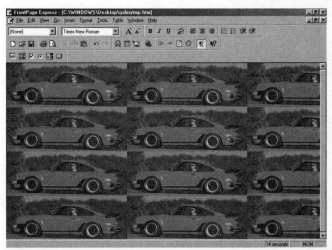

One last option available in the *Background Properties* window worth mentioning is the *Static* checkbox.

If you tick it, the background image will remain static, and only the text will move. If you leave the box uncrossed, you will be able scroll up and down your page with your browser scroll bars. Text and image will move together. This is the default setting.

`Delete an image`

To delete an image, select it with the mouse. Resizing handles will appear, and the image will be displayed in reverse video. You can then use either the:

✔ *Delete* keys on the keyboard; or the

✔ *Clear* command in the *Edit* menu.

4. Links – or how to jump from page to page

One of the great joys of visiting a Web page is when the mouse cursor turns into a small white hand indicating the presence of a link, instantly making you wonder what lies waiting to be discovered at the end of it.

Hypertext links are the foundation of browsing on the Internet and make the whole business of surfing a lot of fun.

A link in a Web page is a simple and instant way of taking you to another Web page in the same document, or site, or to another site anywhere on the Web. 'Linked' documents add variety to the contents of a page and can consist of text, images, sound, etc. They give you access to all the treasures of the Web, making it truly interactive. You can create different types of links, each with its own function and specific features. They can all be inserted in a Web page created with FrontPage Express.

A distinction is usually drawn between 'internal' links, used to browse within the same page, and 'external' links, which connect to other pages of the same site, or target other sites.

The principle of internal and external links is basically the same.

Insert an external link

A hypertext link can connect to a page on the same site, or on another site. In the first case, you can be sure you will end up in a link as it is your own site, but in the second, you have to exercise greater caution. Make sure you check that the site actually exists. A link to a phantom page does your own site no credit at all.

Having said that, linking your pages to other sites is a way of connecting them to the entire network, and of doing justice to the whole principle of the Internet. Your site should preferably not be the last stop in a visitor's browsing, but a link (hopefully an important one) in a chain.

Note

There are companies today that make payments to the authors of sites whose links lead to their pages. It can be quite a lucrative way of earning a living.

To insert a link to another page

You can turn any selection on a page (a character string, an image, etc.) into a link.

 Once you have made your selection, open the link creation window or click on the corresponding icon in the Toolbar.

Create Hyperlink   ✕

Open Pages | World Wide Web | New Page

Open Pages:

    911
    form
    galery
    histo
    index

Bookmark: [none]   ▼

Target Frame:

Hyperlink Points To:

| OK | Cancel | Clear | Extended... | Help |

You will have to use one of the three available tabs, depending on whether:

You want to create a link to another page in your site.

In this case, select the *Open Pages* tab. The *Open pages* field lists the different pages opened in FrontPage Express. If the destination page of the link does not appear, exit this window, open the page in question and start the operation again.

Select the page to open when you activate the link and click *OK*.

A message informs you that a link has been created to a local file (i.e. a file on your hard disk, not on a server connected to the Internet). This is normal, because this page has not yet been published on the Web. Click *OK*.

The target page is opened automatically and the link is now operational.

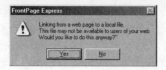

You want to create an internal link to another page on your site, but this page has not yet been created.

In this case in the *New Page* tab, you can follow your link to a page of your site that does not yet exist. Simply give a name to this new page in the *Page Title* field (*Page2*, for example). The URL address of this new page automatically takes this name (*Page2.Htm*), but you can change this if you wish.

Note

You will probably have noticed when you entered the page title that the characters appeared simultaneously in the Page URL . There are some exceptions, however. Some characters are not permitted in Web page titles, either because they correspond to a particular application (the Slash sign [/], for example, means a change of directory), or because they can cause confusion. This is the case with uppercase letters in particular. They are usually avoided when naming pages, as this avoids confusion for the surfer. Basically, it is preferable to keep page titles as simple as possible.

Create Hyperlink				
Open Pages	World Wide Web	New Page		

Page Title: gallery

Page URL: gallery.htm

Target Frame:

Hyperlink Points To: gallery.htm

| OK | Cancel | Clear | Extended... | Help |

When you enter the *Page Title*, FrontPage Express will ask you to choose the type of new page the link is to open. Confirm your choice. A new page is then created and the link will now be active.

You want to create an external link to a page in another site.

In this case select the *World Wide Web* tab.

The *Hyperlink Type* field contains the different Internet protocols (*http* for Web pages, *news* for newsgroups, *mailto* for a link to e-mail boxes, etc.). You can select a type protocol in advance, or type in any address manually.

When you have confirmed your choice, you can still test your link, but this time it will automatically call up your browser and will go to the link automatically if you are connected to the Internet.

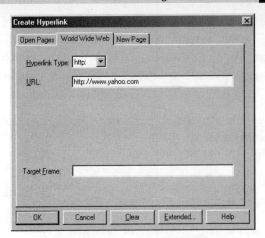

Insert a "Mailto" link

In many cases, you may want the visitors to your site to contact you. If you are running a small business from your site, this facility (called a *Mailto* link) is absolutely essential.

To this end, you must have an e-mail box. An e-mail address can be obtained free of charge from most Internet access providers. If you don't have one already, see the addresses in the appendix for further details.

Creating a link to your e-mail box is no different from creating a link to a Web page. Enter your e-mail address in the *URL* field of the *World Wide Web* tab, and select *mailto:* in the *Hyperlink Type:* field.

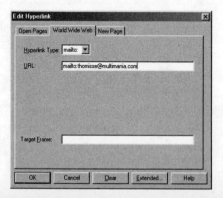

*A mailto link
is available at the
bottom of every
page of our site.*

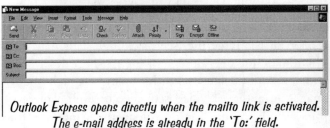

*Outlook Express opens directly when the mailto link is activated.
The e-mail address is already in the 'To:' field.*

⚠ When a Web surfer clicks the *mailto* link, an automatic call to an e-mail application (Outlook Express, for example), will enable him or her to send you a message.

Test the 'Mailto' link from your browser.

Linking to a large file

If you want to enable surfers to download a large file from your site, you can authorise them to access the site, without automatically imposing a restrictive time limit.

The technique consists of giving a small, or 'light', version of the large file (see page 109). This may be a 'thumbnail' picture, an icon or even a short description with a link to the large file, which may be a high-quality image, an audio or video sequence or even a piece of software. To reduce the download time, the large file may be compressed, so you will have to decompress it after you have saved it onto your hard disk.

Many commercial sites use this type of link to entice potential customers. They then ask for a credit card number so that you can pay to receive the complete version of the game, film, or whatever is being sold.

If files are compressed, the person who wishes to download them will have to have a compression/decompression programme that can handle this type of file.

'Zip' files are the most common type of compressed files. Winzip, a compression/decompression shareware application, can be downloaded from the following address:

http://www. winzip. com/WinZip/download. html

Note

You must always keep an eye on the total size of a site containing such files. The servers that offer to publish your site free of charge also impose restrictions on the space your site can take (it is usually limited to a few megabytes). As the market gets more competitive however, this is becoming less of a problem, and you can, of course, spread your site over more than one server to get round any potential difficulties.

Inserting a link to a large file

1 Insert a 'light' version or a description of the complete file into your site, then select it. For example, type in 'To download the film of my first parachute jump (2 Mb, 'zipped'), click here'.

2 Open the Create/Edit link window, using the corresponding icon in the toolbar, the Insert menu, the 'Edit' menu or by pressing <Ctrl> + <K>.

3 Select 'Other' in the 'Hyperlink type' field of the 'World Wide Web' tab.

4 In the 'URL :' field, enter the file access path (which must be in the directory of your Web site), and don't forget to key in the extension of that file ('.zip', '.wav', etc.).

5 Click 'OK' and test the link with your browser.

If the link yields an image, it will be opened in a new window. If it is a sound or video file, the browser will open the appropriate multimedia player.

Finally, when a link is connected to a compressed file, the browser displays a dialogue box which reads *File Download: Open this file from its current location* or *Save it to disk.*

Inserting an anchor

The bookmark, also known as a target or anchor, is an internal link (i.e. within a Web page) that saves you from having to use the scroll bars when the text overruns the bottom of the screen. An anchor is therefore frequently entered at the bottom of the page for an automatic return to the top of the document.

Like a bookmark placed between two pages in a book, the anchor is used to access a predefined point, and therefore to link any point of a text with another. You can use anchors to link, for instance, the different points of a table of contents with the titles of the chapters or paragraphs to which they refer.

A bookmark is inserted and then assigned a link in two steps. You must first create the bookmark and then create the link to it.

Inserting an anchor

Select the target character string, e.g. a title, the name of an image, the beginning of a paragraph, etc. You can place the bookmark at any place where the insertion point (a blinking vertical bar) appears.

Open the 'Edit' menu and select 'Bookmark' to open the bookmark window. The first field, 'Bookmark name,' is self-explanatory. The default entry is the selected text, but you can change this. If other bookmarks have already been placed on the page, they are mentioned in the lower field, so you avoid having two bookmarks with the same name, which may lead to confusion. The 'Clear' button next to this field is used to delete the active bookmark.

If you are satisfied with the settings as they are, click 'OK'. The inserted bookmark is indicated in your page by a blue dashed underline of the pre-selected text. If you did not select characters when you inserted a bookmark, it will be indicated by a small blue flag, which is also visible when the site is published on the Internet.

Bookmarks act in the same way as other links in a browser and the mouse cursor turns into a hand when it
passes over the linked item.

 Creating the link:

Select the text that will serve as a link, or create it if it
does not exist, by entering for example 'Bottom of page,'
if your bookmark refers to the last paragraph of your
page.

Now open the 'Insert' menu and click the
'Hyperlink' command, which can also be accessed with
the shortcut key < Ctrl > + < K >.

The Create Hyperlink window is opened. It has three
tabs, but only the first, 'Open Pages' concerns bookmarks.

The 'Open Pages' field displays the titles of the different
pages on your site. In theory, a link to a bookmark
consists of linking in the same page (which is selected by
default). If this is not the case, select the page to open

when the link connects to the bookmark. In this case, we are no longer dealing with a bookmark strictly speaking, but with an external link.

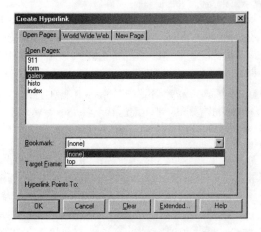

Note: one or more pages?

Is it preferable to divide a Web site into several pages or to have it only on a single page? Unlike a sheet of paper, the length of a Web page is virtually unlimited. So the answer to this question has to be influenced once again by the time it takes to download the files contained within. If your Web site does not contain many large images or documents that take a long time to load, you need not necessarily break it down into several pages. Text is infinitely faster to load than any other type of data (graphics, sound, etc.). Conversely, for a site that contains many images, it is preferable to use multiple pages. In this way, surfers who have loaded the first page of your site can judge for themselves whether they want to visit any further pages or not.

The 'Bookmark' field has a dropdown menu with the different bookmarks created in your page. Select the target bookmark of your link. It will appear in the 'Hyperlink points to' field, preceded by a hash mark (#).

Click 'OK'. The link to the bookmark is now effective. The link is now underlined and has turned blue, the characteristic colour of hypertext links.

Now test the link. Keep the *Ctrl* button pressed and approach the link with the mouse cursor, which now turns into a horizontal arrow. Click to activate the link to the bookmark. The *Follow Hyperlink* command from the *Tools* menu performs the same function. Remember that you can also test the links using your browser.

Clearing links

To clear a link you must edit it. Place your cursor on the link and:

- ✔ Right click it;
- ✔ Open the "Edit" menu, then "Hyperlink,"
- ✔ Open the "Insert" menu then "Hyperlink" or
- ✔ Activate the "Create Hyperlink" command, or
- ✔ Press <Ctrl> and <K> simultaneously.

And you will access the "Create Hyperklink" window. Press the "Clear"button to delete the hyperlink.

5. Musical interludes

Sound is an important part of the multimedia world, yet you will find music on relatively few sites. Aside from sites devoted specifically to music, where you can often download many samples (the 'Mp3' format tops the list here), silence seems to reign supreme on Web.

The reasons for this can be summed up in the three words that spell out the constraints of using multimedia on the Web: compatibility, file size and quality.

Compatibility

Some sound processing packages use their own formats not recognised by all applications of the same type. This problem is exacerbated on the Internet, as the formats managed by the different browsers are not always the same.

The most widespread are '.WAV' files (Windows standard), '.AIFF' files (Macintosh standard) and '.MID' files (used for Musical Instrument Digital Interface). Other more recent, high-performance formats are also widely used on the Net. These require specific plug-ins (additional modules that are 'plugged into' an application to enhance its performance).

Two other formats deserve mention, the '.MP3' (or Mpeg2 Audio Layer3) format, the most widely used audio format of the MPEG audio/video standard, and '.RA' ('RealAudio'), both of which allow you listen to the audio files as they are being downloaded.

The '.WAV' and '.MID' files are managed by Windows Media Player. MP3 files require a program such as Winamp (which can be downloaded free of charge from www.winamp.com) to function, or the latest version of Windows Media Player:

http://www.microsoft.com/windows/windowsmedia/default

To play Real Audio files, you will need to get Real Player from **www.real.com**. Although the deluxe version of this piece of software is not free (it will cost you about US $ 30), you can download a standard version for a 30-day trial period from the same site.

File size

Keep an eye on the size of files. This is one of the Web site designer's golden rules. The size of Audio files often dissuades people from including them on their Web sites. A two-second Wav file takes up about 20 KB of memory, while a one-minute MIDI file takes up two thirds of that space.

For large files, the '.MP3' and 'Real Audio' formats are the most widespread. Bear in mind that a minute of music compressed in MP3 takes up about 1 MB.

Quality

MIDI files play back information using the computer's internal sound card. The quality of the sound card therefore determines the quality of playback.

WAV files can be of varying quality and depend on the recording quality.

The MP3 and Real Audio formats offer the best size for quality ratio, but whatever format you use, do not expect CD quality sound.

Inserting a sound

If you are using Internet Explorer as your browser, you can insert background sound on any Web page using FrontPage Express. The selected sound can be repeated a specified number of times or played in an endless loop. The size of your site will not suffer as a result, as sound is loaded only once by the visitor to the site. On the other hand, an endless loop may become really annoying in the long term, especially if it is short and therefore very repetitive. See the note on page 147 if you want this feature to work and you are using Netscape's 'Navigator' browser.

In the *Insert* menu, click the *Background Sound* command and then the *Browse* option next to the *From File* field. Use Windows Explorer to find the file you want to insert and select it. The background sound is inserted without requesting confirmation, giving you the impression that nothing happened. You can check whether or not it has worked by visiting the site using your browser.

Note

If the audio file inserted does not have a ".wav" or ".mid" extension, create a link to a site where your visitor can download the required plug in.

If you open the Page Properties window (through the *File* menu or by right clicking on the page), you will find that the access path to the file is entered in the *Location* field under *Background sound* area.

Once you have chosen a background sound, you can customise it using two options:

Loop, where you can have the sound played from '0' to '9999' times in a row, and

Forever – which is self-explanatory.

Recording your own sounds

Once again, there are legions of sound recording and mixing software applications. You have to pay for most of them and each can support a certain variety of formats. Some require specific hardware, others can work with the standard hardware of a multimedia computer. All have their own specific features.

The Windows Sound Recorder can be used to record sounds from an auxiliary peripheral such as a microphone, which must be connected to the sound card of your computer. Before you proceed, however, remember that you should abide by the copyright laws, which apply on the World Wide Web just as they do in the non-virtual world.

To insert a link to an audio file

Thanks to the links you provide, a visitor to your site will be able to listen to a sound upon request. In this case, your file compatibility and size problems are solved, in that you can inform the visitor of the characteristics of the file without imposing a format (the quality is still a matter of the format used). You should therefore write a brief description (e.g. 'Click here to listen to my latest composition, in X format and Y minutes long'), select this text and then insert the link as already described (see 'Inserting a link to a large-size file' page 130).

Internet Explorer and Netscape Communicator

In spite of all precautions regarding the compatibility of sound formats between different browsers, one serious constraint remains; the HTML tag needed to insert a background sound in Microsoft products (Word, FrontPage, etc.) is not recognised by Netscape, the direct competitor of MS Internet Explorer. As nearly all Internet users use one of these two browsers, this is by no means a negligible inconvenience.

If confronted by this problem, try the following:

When an audio file is inserted in FrontPage Express, the following tag is introduced in the HTML code of the Web page: BGSOUND SRC= . This tag is not recognised by Netscape. On the other hand, the tag used by the latter browser, EMBED SRC= , is recognised by Internet Explorer, and is considered to be universal.

All you have to do to solve the problem therefore is replace BGSOUND by EMBED in the HTML code.

Click the HTML command in the View menu. A window will display the entire code of the page.

The BGSOUND tag is usually in the first lines of code. Delete this character string (as you would do in any word processor), replace it with EMBED and click OK .

Since FrontPage Express does not recognise the standard tag of the Windows system ('BGSOUND'), a plug-in that can manage it is automatically inserted (Windows Media Player Control). It appears as a thumbnail which looks like a connecting plug. This image will remain visible on your page, but you can hide it using the *Plug-in Properties* dialogue box, by a right mouse click or through the *Edit* menu. Once viewed using a browser, the plug-in will be invisible.

5

The other components of a Web site

The other components of a Web site

You should now be capable of creating a basic Web site, containing many lines of text in a varied and attractive layout, adding images in GIF or JPEG format, perhaps a table, a background image or even some background sound. Ideally there should be a number of hyperlinks in your pages, internal links to make browsing within the site an easy and pleasant experience and external ones to guide the visiting surfer to other addresses. If your site is interesting and has character then visitors will remember it and want to come back, and better still, maybe tell their friends to visit also. In that case, what more could you ask?

Some finishing touches, more variety, a little more zest perhaps?

There are some other functions available in FrontPage Express that have not yet been discussed.

Images that move

Everything is in motion; everything is alive on the Web. The whole concept of hypertext is a device that turns information into something that is not static, but always on the move. The Web is awash with banners, scrolling text, animated GIFS, Java scripts, Flash animation, etc. The Web today is decidedly cinematic. However, there are still drawbacks. The Web is limited by the amount of memory available on the computers of those who use it. It therefore requires images, sound and other data that do not take up too much memory, and consequently, load in a short space of time. Although animation can bring a site to life, it can also make sites heavy and slow and therefore completely off-putting to the visitor.

Consequently, although animation is everywhere on the Web, it often takes the form of small-size images, highly compressed in a reduced format, consisting of loops of just a few images.

Animated GIFs

As their name implies, animated GIFs are animated files of several small images in GIF format, often very small in size and extremely simple. They are intended first and foremost to attract attention. *Click here* often alternates with one or two images that highlight the link. Other, more gratuitous animated sequences, are intended solely to enrich a site and make it more attractive. Advertising has invaded the Web in a major way, but the proliferation of advertisements on sites does illustrate how effective animated GIFS are considered to be.

There is an infinite variety of animated GIFS on the Web. A large number of them are in the public domain and you can use them as you like (see addresses in the Appendix).

Creating small pieces of animation is not such a daunting prospect as you might at first think, but it does lie outside the scope of this book. It also requires specialised software, (for instance, Microsoft Gif Animator, a Freeware program you can download from http://mssjus1.www.conxion.com/msdownload/gifanimator/gifsetup.exe).

Inserting an animated GIF with FrontPage Express

Inserting an animated GIF in FrontPage Express is no different from inserting a static image on your Web page (see 'Decorating your Web page', page 95).

Place the insertion point where you want the animation to appear on your page. Open the Insert menu and click the *Image* command (or on the icon in the Toolbar). Click the *Browse* button next to the *From File* field. Enter the Animated GIF in your site's directory and click *OK*. The animated GIF is inserted instantly. You can change its properties, but as these files are usually small in size, it makes little sense to seek alternative ways to display them.

Web, live and videotape

Unlike small animated files such as animated GIFs, video (digitised real images) takes up an alarming amount of memory because it requires high definition, a large number of images and a large number of colours. As in the case of photography, compression can speed up download times, but can also dramatically alter the video quality.

Videos currently available on the Web still tend to be of mediocre quality, which is surprising given the lengthy time they take to download.

Note

By way of example, it can take nearly hour to download a simple advertising trailer from a feature film.

The disconcerting number of formats also causes serious compatibility problems. To avoid the need to use endless plug-ins, four standards are normally used:

AVI (**Audio Video Interleave**): not very compressed, this is the most widely used standard under Windows. It is handled by Windows Media Player, which is installed in all computers running Windows 95 (or above). The latest version of this software can be downloaded free of charge from:

http://www.microsoft.com/

QuickTime and Movie: QuickTime (extention .qt) is the Macintosh video standard. Adapted under Windows, it gave rise to the .MOV format.

The .Mov and .qt formats can also be handled by the Microsoft Media Player, but the most recent QuickTime files require a QuickTime drive. A basic version of this software is available free of charge (the complete version is called QuickTime Pro) from:

http://www.quicktime.apple.com

MPEG (Moving Pictures coding Experts Group): the most successful format on the Web. Reliable and compact, it is now emerging as the industry standard, to the point that some digital video cameras can now film directly in this format. The most widespread version on the Web is MPEG2, although MPEG7 was recently released. Version 2 can be read by the Microsoft Windows Media Player 2.

RealVideo (part of the Real Audio package): this format from RealNetworks has the best speed for quality ratio in streaming.

Streaming

This is technology used for loading images in small packets, so that a video sequence can be viewed directly without having to wait for the complete file to load. QuickTime 3 videos also feature this function.

If the quality cannot rival that of the other formats mentioned, the many other advantages of streaming have made the RealVideo format very popular on the Web. RealVideo and the RealPlayer G2 can be downloaded from:

http://www.real.com

To sum up, if you want to insert a video on your Web site, make sure that your file format is one of these standards. Try to obtain a good compression rate for quality, but don't expect miracles. Finally, avoid long sequences and excessively large image dimensions (never exceed 320 x 240 pixels).

Inserting a video sequence with FrontPage Express

1. Open the Insert menu and click 'Video'.

2. Go to your site's directory. Select the source file and click 'OK'.

3. The video sequence is inserted automatically, but appears only as a small black frame on the screen.

4. This is obviously not the real size of your video. To preview the sequence, go to your browser, open the page of your site that contains the video file and take a look.

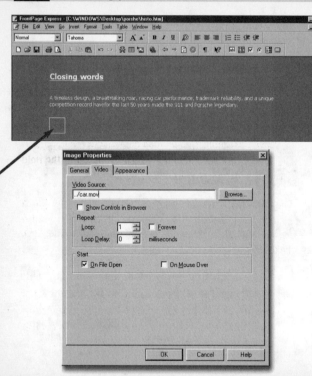

5 Right click on the frame to access the 'Image Properties' window (or go via the 'Edit' menu).

6 The 'Video' tab is selected by default, and contains several options:

 'Loop' is used to set the number of times the sequence is to be played, once, several or infinitely (in which case tick Forever). The loop delay (between one thousandth of a second and 10 seconds) is set in the field of the same name ('Loop delay').

 The 'Start' field is used to define when your video will start. Select either 'On File Open' or 'On Mouse Over', i.e. when your page is opened, or when the visitor's cursor passes over the first image of the sequence.

The 'General' and 'Appearance' tabs fulfil the same functions as for a fixed image. You can, for instance, write descriptive text on the content of the video sequence for the benefit of your visitors.

Inserting a form

Forms are an effective means of obtaining information about the surfers who visit your pages. You can find out who is connected to your site, how and why they ended up there and most importantly, what they think of it.

Unlike official forms (which must be filled in when registering with a service provider, or when shopping on line), you cannot force your visitors to answer your questions. Nevertheless, many surfers will do so willingly.

With FrontPage Express, you can create a form in many different ways, depending on personal preferences, the time you want to devote to the task and so on.

Once you have got the hang of customised forms, you will be able to use the form creation wizard and the pre-formatted forms to be found in FrontPage Express without any problem.

Custom form

The *Form Field* menu features the constituent elements of a form. These elements can also be inserted using the relevant icons in the *Form* Toolbar.

Click the respective icon to insert, from left to right:

1. A line of simple text.
2. An area of scrolling text.
3. A checkbox.
4. A radio button.
5. A dropdown menu.
6. A command button.

Each of them will have to be preceded or followed by relevant comments.

Creating a table may prove very helpful when it comes to formatting the different constituent elements of the form.

The different form fields

Let us now go over the various elements that can be used to compose a form :

One-Line Text Box :

As its name implies, this field will contain information entered on a single line.

Each form field has its own properties, which can be changed using the *Form Field Properties,* accessible via the shortcut or the *Edit menu.* If you have time, test the various settings of each of the following fields yourself.

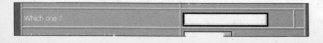

Scrolling Text Box :

The advantage of a scrolling text box is that it can contain a large amount of text in a minimum space. Information is scrolled in it using the horizontal and vertical scroll bars. It often contains contractual clauses and other such types of text, which, though of prime importance, tend to run to several pages. Scrolling text boxes in Web pages can also include optional texts of secondary importance. This is a tactful way of not imposing such information on your visitors.

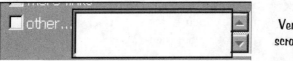

Vertical
scroll bar

Check Box :

A 'check box' can perform many functions. In general, these boxes need not be ticked and there are many possible choices for a list.

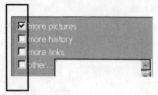

Radio button :

Unlike a checkbox, a radio button allows you to select only one choice among several options. It is used frequently for questions such 'What is your age bracket?'

Drop-Down Menu :

Dropdown menus contain several options. They perform the same function as radio buttons or checkboxes, but they save a lot of space, which can be important when the available options are numerous. They are frequently used for such questions as 'Occupation?' (one choice only is usually required) or 'Hobbies' (several choices are possible).

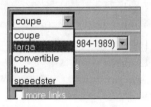

Push button:

Push buttons are placed at the end of the form and are usually attributed two functions: *Submit*, which when clicked sends the results to the relevant address, and *Reset*, which resets the default values of the form so that users can start again from scratch. The latter of the buttons is optional, but *Submit* must appear in every form without fail.

Form properties

The *Form Properties* are accessed from the Shortcut menu or the Edit menu. You enter the name of your form and the address to which the completed form is be submitted. Several fields have to be completed in the *Form Properties* window:

1. In the 'Form Handler' field, you must retain the default settings 'Custom ISAPI, NSAPI or GI Script'.

2. In the 'Form Name', you enter the name of your form.

   Leave the other fields blank.

3. Now click the 'Settings' button next to the 'Form Name' field to access the 'Settings for Custom Form Finder' window.

4. In the 'Action' field, indicate first the type of action the browser is to carry out when sending information contained in the form; this is a 'Mailto' action, i.e. a link to an e-mail box.

   Enter 'mailto :', followed by your e-mail address:

5. Keep the default settings of the 'Method' field ('Post', which indicates the sending of a message by e-mail).

6. You can leave the 'Coding type :' field blank.

7. Click 'OK', then 'OK' again in the 'Form Properties' window.

Your form is finally ready, so you will soon be in a position to know more about the anonymous surfers who come and visit your site. When they have completed the different fields of the form and clicked the button to submit it, the following window will warn them about the risks of sending confidential data.

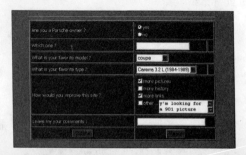

Once the submitted form is accepted, the results will reach you after a few minutes, appearing as a new message in your e-mail box. This message, entitled 'Form submitted by … (your visitor's browser name)' is a list, where each line comprises the title of a field from the questionnaire followed by the reply entered by the user, or present in the form. How clear the replies are will depend largely on how you have labelled the different fields of your form. The results can then be used by a database software package or spreadsheet (in Microsoft Excel, for example).

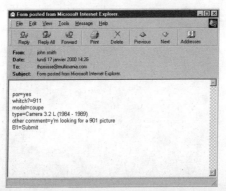

6

Publishing your site on the Internet

Publishing your site on the Internet

Introduction :

You've made it – hopefully by now you have created your first Web page, so all that remains to do is to get it published.

Like a writer who has spent long months putting the finishing touches to his latest novel, you will now have to look for an editor, someone to take on the job of actually getting your page out there in the public eye. In the world of the Web, a 'host' performs the role of the book world's editor. In a matter of minutes, your new site can join the millions of others that make up the Web, and constitute a new link in the chain that daily connects more and more surfers in every corner of the globe.

Publishing is neither difficult nor costly and can take as little as half an hour, but you do need to be able to concentrate. The slightest distraction can derail the process and backtracking to pinpoint the fatal error may prove extremely tiresome, so follow the instructions carefully step by step and be patient.

What exactly is a host ?

There are a plethora of terms alongside that of host, such as access provider, server and service provider, which can get very confusing for the uninitiated. Access providers and service providers refer to computers that provide (free of charge or otherwise) connection to the Internet, together with several services such as Newsgroups, e-mail addresses and also the option of hosting Web pages. The host is the server that publishes your Web pages. A server is any computer connected constantly to the Internet, to which surfers can connect to access the information the Internet contains. Therefore, a server is not exactly the same thing as an access provider, although there is a tendency to use the two terms indiscriminately.

So, to be precise, a host is a server computer that provides free space on its hard disk to each of its subscribers. Space is not unlimited, which is understandable when you think of all the thousands of people out there, probably pondering the creation of their own Web site even as you read this, and you can imagine the storage capacity needed by a server that hosts tens of thousands of sites.

Hosting on the service provider's site

If you have embarked on creating your personal Web site, you are probably already connected to the Internet, and thus have a subscription to an access provider. However, when you chose this provider you may have neglected to ask a very important question - does it host Web sites?

If the answer is no, then don't worry. You can easily use the services of another provider. Simply do a little research on the best provider for you and complete the relevant subscription form.

You don't need to search long and hard nowadays to find free access to the Internet. Competition between the different providers is already fierce and is getting fiercer as their numbers grow by the day. Some Internet providers are now also offering free Internet calls, in addition to free access to the Web.

A list of some such free Internet connections is given in the Appendix. See also the address below:

http://thelist.internet.com

How to choose your provider

Just because you can get free access to the Internet does not mean you cannot be demanding. Quite the opposite in fact. You should be able to take your pick of the providers, so make sure you select the right one for you. Here are a few things to consider when making your decision.

Cost: why pay for the service when there are so many possibilities to get access for free?

However, free access is one thing, but those phone bills do tend to add up so do check if the potential provider is also offering free time online.

Speed: the Internet connection speed depends on the type of line your provider uses (cable, satellite, ADSL, etc.) and the modem you use. The best way to judge this speed is to test it.

Allocated space: how much space can your site have on your provider's hard disk? This varies on average from 5 to 15 MB.

Geographic location: telephone charges are often dependant on the time of day or night you connect to the Internet. More people will try to go online during off-peak hours which tends to clutter it up. Study your time brackets carefully. If your site is hosted in the US, your server will probably be saturated when Europeans want to connect to it during off-peak hours.

Hotline: a hotline is telephone support provided by a service provider to help if you have a problem. Does your provider have a hotline? Is it available round the clock? What rates do they charge? Be careful, as the charges can be exorbitant at times.

Reputation: finally, a good reputation often goes hand in hand with quality. Talk to your friends, read the trade press and generally be an informed consumer.

Even if you already have an Internet subscription, these few tips may prompt you to switch providers.

Free hosting service on a specialised site

Some sites provide free space for the publication of Web pages, without necessarily offering access to the Internet. They are not access providers, only hosts. All you have to do is complete a form and the space will be provided for your pages.

Once you have enrolled, you will usually be sent an e-mail confirmation message. You usually have to return it (by clicking on a link) to confirm your enrolment. You should print out this e-mail message, because it contains all the information you will need afterwards.

You now have the space you need to host your Web site. A homepage will already be featured on it. It usually includes your identifier name and perhaps a banner stating 'site under construction'.

Connect to the address of this page to have a look. Congratulations! Your site is now on the Web.

Example of a site under construction
at freeservers.com.

> ### Note
>
> In return for hosting your site, you will often be asked to accept a small advertising marquee on your site.

 Choose your host carefully. The selection criteria for a provider apply to a hosting site too.

Addresses of sites offering to host Web pages free of charge are included in the Appendix.

Transfering your Web page onto the page server

The first thing to do when transferring your site to the host site is to conduct some last-minute checks. Ideally you should double-check everything. Go through the same routine you would use if you were about to go on holiday. Did you pack your toothbrush? Is there enough petrol in the car, etc.

Use your browser to test your site once again offline and make sure that all the files of your site are in the same folder. Check the total size of your site too, as it might restrict your choice of host.

Finally, name your Home page 'Index.htm' or 'Index.html'. This restriction is imposed by most hosts. When you transfer files, you will be asked to name the first page in a certain way to tell the server which page refers to the address of your site. This name might not be 'Index'. It all depends on your server. In any event, the required title is clearly indicated.

HTML or HTM ?

There is no basic difference between files with extension .htm or .html . Both actually designate the same format. .htm is used by computers whose operating system (usually Dos) will not accept file format names with the second part exceeding three letters.

When you have finished all this checking and double-checking, you are ready for the big moment. You are about to unleash your site on an unsuspecting world.

To transfer a site onto the hard disk of a host server you will have to use a data transfer protocol known as FTP, which stands for File Transfer Protocol. FTP can be used not only to download files on your hard disk from any Web site, but also to reverse the process, i.e. transfer files (a Web site for instance) from your computer to the hard disk of a server.

This operation requires an FTP client or downloading module, i.e. file transfer software. Some Web page editors have their own transfer modules. Since FrontPage Express does not, you can get one of these programmes and use it as a linked publishing program. Downloading an FTP client from the Web is no problem once again. These programmes are quite numerous, most often shareware and are relatively small in size (about 1 MB on average), so they will take only a few minutes to download. A list of sites where they can be obtained is included in the Appendix.

Every Web page hosting site will urge you to download a transfer module. Cue FTP and FTP Expert, both of which are shareware, and are frequently used. We would advise you to use the software offered by your host, because you will have the benefit of a help feature that will explain to you how it works and offer step-by-step instructions on how to publish your site.

We published our site '911' using FTP Expert, the FTP client from Visicom Media. This program is incredibly easy to use. Your site will be downloaded to your host server in a few minutes.

7

Maintaining and promoting your personal site

Maintaining and promoting your own site

Register your Web page with search engines

On the Web, a site is like a needle in a haystack. Hundreds of thousands of new sites are added everyday and the Web grows ever denser and more chaotic, to the extent that it is turning into a gigantic bazaar. How on earth is anyone ever going to find your site therefore? The answer is, with a search engine.

Search engines are detective robots, the cybernetic counterparts of Sherlock Holmes with unbelievable capacities. They are, in fact, computer programmes that labour relentlessly to cross-reference the new arrivals on the Web, classifying them into fields and categories to form gigantic databases. To use them, you simply enter one or more keywords and they will produce a list of all the sites whose 'classification record' contains the terms of the query.

Getting your site listed consists of going to as many search engines or directories as possible and registering with them. See the list of the most popular search engines, contained in the Appendix and also 'Search Engines', another title in this series.

Open wide and say 'ah'

The Web is at your service, and will bend over backwards to please you. It will even carry out a little check-up on your Web page free of charge. Contact one of the many 'doctors' on duty round the clock on the Web, to examine your baby.

Here is a non-exhaustive list of the types of examination these electronic doctors will perform on your page:

They will:

✓ Test your pages for Meta-tags (special tags providing information about what's in the Web page [keyword, author, etc.]) and note down what they contain;

✓ Calculate the size and loading time of the different pages;

✓ Register your site in several search engines;

✓ Check for sites with links to your pages;

✓ Check for HTML syntax errors;

✓ Verify whether your site is compatible with the different browsers.

A Help function is often available so that you can improve your results. Remember to wait a few days before you use these diagnostic tools, to give the search engines time to integrate your pages correctly into their databases.

The addresses of these Web page testers are given in the Appendices.

8

Appendices

Appendix 1: Glossary

Access provider: A company that provides (free or paying) access to the Internet and other types of related services (e-mail address, Web site hosting, etc.).

Account: Data necessary to benefit from a service. For example, a subscription account with an Internet access-provider includes the server's dial-up number, your user-name, your password.

ADSL: Abbreviation for *Asymmetric Digital Subscriber Line*. ADSL is a new technology enabling connections about 30 times faster than by normal telephone call.

Animated GIF : Image containing several images in GIF format following one another to create an animation. The animation can be viewed in an Internet browser.

ASCII : American Standard for Information Interchange. A 'computerised' alphabet (code) used to represent all alphanumeric characters.

Bit: Abbreviation for Binary Digit. The bit is the smallest unit of information. A bit may only have the value 1 or 0.

Bookmark : Internal link to a Web page.

Bps: Abbreviation for Bits per second.

Browser: Program making it possible to view Web pages (and their contents). The most popular are Internet Explorer and Netscape Navigator.

Client: Computer accessing a server.

Connect: the action of joining the Internet. A modem is generally necessary to connect up.

Downloading: Retrieving files or Web pages from another computer connected to Internet into your computer.

E-mail : Electronic mail transmitted via the Internet.

File: A file contains computer data. It may contain any kind of information: text, images, a program. A file is always characterised by a name and an extension. For example: cloud.jpg is a file containing an image.

Flash: Program making it possible to make animations and interactive presentations that can be viewed in a Web page. They can be viewed with the aid of the plug-in Shockwave.

Freeware : Software given away for free.

FTP: File Transfer Protocol. Protocol used to transfer files on the Internet.

GIF: Abbreviation for Graphic Interchange Format – compressed image format. See also JPEG and Animated GIF.

Home page : The first page loaded when connecting to a Web site.

Host : Server that hosts Web sites.

HTML: Abbreviation for HyperText Markup Language. HTML is the language used to create the pages on the Internet. Among other things, HTML makes it possible to create hypertext links.

HTTP: Abbreviation for *HyperText Transfer Protocol*. Protocol for transferring HTML files and elements linked to them (images, animations, etc.). See also HTTP Server.

HTTP Server: An HTTP server puts sites (made up of HTML files) and the elements of which they are composed (images, Java applets, etc.) at the disposal of Surfers.

Hypertext: Text containing links taking you either to another place in the same page or to another page. All the HTML pages in the Internet, as well as most of the Help files, make use of hypertext.

Internet address: Address assigned to a site. For example: http://www.yahoo.com.

Internet Service Provider: Firm providing access to Internet by subscription.

IP address: *Abbreviation for Interconnection Protocol.* The IP address is a series of four numbers assigned to every computer connected on the Internet in order to identify them. These four numbers range from 0 to 255. There is a textual address for each IP address, which is easier to memorise. For example: 206.132.15.12 is the IP address of the Encyclopaedia Britannica. Its textual address is http://www.britannica.com.

ISDN: Abbreviation for *Integrated Services Digital Network.* ISDN is a completely digital network. It is capable of transmitting speech or computer data along telephone lines at a maximum speed of 128 KB/sec. See also ADSL and Cable Modem.

Java: Programming language recognised by all the latest browsers. It makes it possible to insert animations, interactivity, sound, etc. See also Java Applet and JavaScript.

JavaScript: Program in Java language written directly in an HTML page. See also: Java Applet.

JPEG: Abbreviation for Joint Photographic Expert Group. Compressed image format. See also GIF.

Link: In a hypertext document (a Web page, for example) this will take you to another page, another file, an email address. A link can take you almost anywhere.

Login: Name assigned to you to access a server (for example, to connect you to the Internet).

Mailto : Link to an e-mail address.

Modem: Abbreviation for *Modulator-Demodulator*. A modem makes it possible to get connected to the Internet via a traditional telephone line. When leaving the computer the numeric data is converted into analogue data (modulation) appropriate for travelling over the telephone network. When coming in to the receiving computer, the analogue data is converted back (demodulation).

Multimedia : Multimedia computers are used to present different types of information (text, images, sound). The Web is a multimedia universe.

Netiquette : Contraction of "(Inter)Net" and etiquette. Netiquette describes the ethics of the Net: it defines the rules of good behaviour on the Internet. You will find it at the following address: http://www.dtcc.edu/cs/rfc1855.html.

Network: A network is a group of computers linked together. The Internet is a network.

Plug-in: Small program added to a software program to give it extra functions. *Shockwave*, for example, is a plug-in for Internet browsers: it enables Flash animations to be displayed.

Protocol: Rules defining the manner in which data is transmitted between two computers – for example, HTTP is the transfer protocol for Web page data.

Provider : See "Access provider."

Search Engine : Specialised program that searches Internet addresses for specified keywords.

Secured page: Transmits information securely on the Web, (for example, a credit-card number) between your computer and a server. The protocol most often used is SSL.

Server: Computer providing a specific service on any kind of network (including the Internet). The computer that accesses a server is called a client. For example: an HTTP server.

Site: Collection of Web pages containing text and multimedia elements. It is accessed through an address typed into a browser.

Surfing: Using a browser to visit sites on the Internet.

Text file: File containing text without layout (bold, justification, italics, etc.)

URL: Abbreviation for Uniform Resource Locator. See Internet Address .

WebMaster: The webmaster is the individual responsible for a site. He is usually the one who created it.

World Wide Web: The World Wide Web groups all the Web pages of all the Internet sites together.

Wysiwyg : What you see is what you get. Said of a software program that enables you to see the document on the display screen exactly the way it will appear when published.

Appendix 2: Internet addresses

Free access to the Internet

http://www.freedomi.com   http://www.freecall-uk.com

Free e-mail address

http://edit.my.yahoo.com   http ://www.hotmail.com

Shareware – FTP Clients

Cute FTP : http://www.cuteftp.com

Freewares and sharewares

http://www.tucows.com

Free hosting

http://www.topcities.com   http://www.fortunecity..com
http://www.freeservers.com

Animated GIFs and other graphics

http://www.freegraphicland.com/index.html
http://clip-art.freestuffcenter.com

Miscellaneous software

Gif animator : http://mssjus3.www.conxion.com/msdownload/gifanima-
tor/gifsetup.exe

Mediaplayer : http://www.microsoft.com/windows/windowsmedia/default.htm

Quicktime : http://www.quicktime.apple.com

Winzip : http://www.winzip.com/WinZip/download.html

Search engines

http://www.lycos.com   http://www.altavista.com

http://www.yahoo.com

Browsers

http://www.microsoft.com/windows/ie/default.htm

http://www.netscape.com

Referencing your site

http://www.addme.com

http://register-it.netscape.com

Testing your site

http://www.netmechanic.com

For free

http://free.com

Index